WEREWOLVES

BY JIM OLLHOFF

VISIT US AT
WWW.ABDOPUBLISHING.COM

Editors: John Hamilton/Tad Bornhoft
Graphic Design: Sue Hamilton
Cover Design: Neil Klinepier
Cover Illustration: *Leap* ©1981 Don Maitz
Interior Photos and Illustrations: p 1 Henry Hull from *Werewolf of London*, Corbis; pp 4-5 *Orphan* ©1979 Don Maitz; pp 6-7 Wolf howling, Corbis; p 8 Werewolf drawing, Corbis; p 9 Werewolf drawing, Corbis; p 10 Viennese postcard, Corbis; p 11 Actress Maria Ouspenskaya as Maleva in *The Wolf Man*, Corbis; pp 12-13 Wolf howling, Corbis; p 14 Wolfsbane flower, Photo Researchers, Inc.; p 15 Snarling gray wolf, Corbis; p 16 Human aggression wolfman, Photo Researchers, Inc.; p 17 Romulus and Remus statue, Corbis; p 18 *Leap* ©1981 Don Maitz; p 20 Boy with hypertrichosis, AP/Wideworld; p 21 Man in a wolf mask, AP/Wideworld; p 22 Jack Nicholson from *Wolf*, Corbis; p 23 top left: *I Was a Teenage Werewolf* poster, courtesy American International Pictures; top right: Actor Michael Landon in *I Was a Teenage Werewolf*, Corbis; middle left: *Werewolf of London* poster, Corbis; middle right: Actor Henry Hull in *Werewolf of London*; Getty Images; bottom left: *An American Werewolf in London*, courtesy Universal Pictures, Inc.; bottom right: Actor David Naughton in *An American Werewolf in London*, courtesy Universal Pictures, Inc.; p 24 Wolf howls at orange moon, Photo Researchers, Inc.; p 25 Two wolves interacting, Photo Researchers, Inc.; p 26 Snarling wolf, Photo Researchers, Inc.; p 27 Reenactors wearing wolf pelts, Corbis; p 28 U.S. postage stamp of Lon Chaney, Jr., courtesy United States Postal Service; p 29 Wolf in snow at night, Corbis; p 31 Black wolf pup, courtesy Barry O'Neill, National Park Service, U.S. Department of the Interior; p 32 Wolf, ©2001 John Hamilton.

Library of Congress Cataloging-in-Publication Data

Ollhoff, Jim, 1959-
Werewolves / Jim Ollhoff.
    p. cm. -- (The world of horror)
Includes index.
ISBN-13: 978-1-59928-775-1
ISBN-10: 1-59928-775-7
1. Werewolves. I. Title.

GR830.W4O55 2007
398.24'54--dc22
                                        2006032734

CONTENTS

THE HOWL AT MIDNIGHT

Sally was afraid to be out so late at night. Now she couldn't find her way back to her farm. The thick forest brush made walking very hard, and she couldn't tell if she was on the path. It was almost midnight. The light of the full moon shone through the trees, making eerie shadows on the ground. Suddenly, a howl pierced the quiet of the forest. She knew what a wolf sounded like, but this was different. The deep, other-worldly howl sent shivers down the young girl's spine.

Sally called for her older brother, Jason. A minute ago she thought she'd seen him just up ahead on the path. Sally was concerned about Jason. A few weeks earlier, a wild animal had bitten him, and he just hadn't been the same since. Jason said it might have been a wolf that bit him, but he wasn't sure. Ever since the attack, he had acted more alert, more nervous, and more aggressive. His ears could detect the slightest sound. Even more odd, all the farm animals were now afraid of him. Whenever Jason approached, the animals tried to run away.

Right: Orphan, an illustration by fantasy artist Don Maitz.

Two nights ago, Jason had disappeared. Now the whole village was out looking for him. At dusk Sally thought she had seen him in the distance. She called out and ran toward him, but he never answered or turned around. He ran faster than she'd ever seen a person run. He vanished into the forest, and Sally couldn't keep up. Before she realized it, she was deep in the dark woods, and the sun was setting fast.

Now, after losing sight of Jason, Sally realized she was lost. She called for her brother, but she heard only the wind. She stood there a minute, shivering in the night air, listening. Suddenly, the hair on the back of her neck stood up—a large animal hidden behind the trees started growling. It was a rumbling noise that shook the earth upon which Sally stood.

Something moved in the shadows. Was it a wolf? Or was it her brother? Sally was sure she saw an animal lurching forward on its hind legs. "Jason," she called out softly. "Is that you?" There was no response—it was a wolf.

Or was it?

WHAT IS A WEREWOLF?

The word *werewolf* means "man-wolf." It comes from an ancient language called *Anglo-Saxon,* which was spoken by the people who lived in and around England between the 5th and 11th centuries. A werewolf is a legendary creature that can change from a human being into a wolf, and then back again. Some legends say the light of the full moon triggers this change.

Of all the legendary beasts and monsters, werewolves are the most savage. They attack for no reason, and they bite with no mercy. Werewolves seek only to destroy their prey.

A few hundred years ago, many people believed in werewolves. The belief grew especially strong in Europe. When the moon was full and wolf howls filled the forest, people stayed home behind locked doors where it was safe.

In countries that didn't have many wolves, legends emerged about other animals. People in India used to be afraid of vicious were-tigers—people who could change into tigers, and then back into human form. In Africa, people feared the dreaded were-leopards, or were-lions. In South America, people were always on the lookout for the dangerous were-jaguars.

In North America, some Native American cultures held the tradition of the skin-walkers—people who could change into different animals, including wolves. Other places have stories about were-snakes, were-bears, and even were-pigs!

Above & *Facing Page: Werewolf,* a 17th-century illustration by Charles Le Brunoe.

Becoming a Werewolf

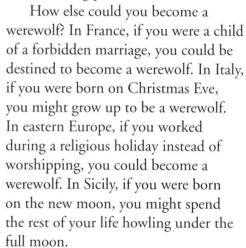

Below: A 1911 postcard illustrating a Viennese story called *The Werewolf.*

Hundreds of werewolf legends, myths, and folktales have been told all over the world. So, there isn't just one way to become a werewolf. There are dozens of ways in which people become werewolves—it all depends on the legend, and the country from which the legend began.

The most common way of becoming a werewolf is to get bitten by one. Most of us know about this because many movies and stories have shown the dreaded bite as the starting point for werewolfism.

How else could you become a werewolf? In France, if you were a child of a forbidden marriage, you could be destined to become a werewolf. In Italy, if you were born on Christmas Eve, you might grow up to be a werewolf. In eastern Europe, if you worked during a religious holiday instead of worshipping, you could become a werewolf. In Sicily, if you were born on the new moon, you might spend the rest of your life howling under the full moon.

According to some traditions, you became a werewolf as a curse from someone else. If you managed to annoy a gypsy or a witch, they might get revenge by turning you into a werewolf. Legend has it that the famous Christian saint of Ireland, Saint Patrick (415-493 A.D.), turned an unlucky British chieftain into a werewolf.

Above: Actress Maria Ouspenskaya portrays the character Maleva from the 1941 film *The Wolf Man*. Maleva was famous for saying, "Even a man who says his prayers by night may become a werewolf at the full moon."

Above: A wolf howls in the twilight.

According to some legends, you became a werewolf if you had some kind of interaction with a wolf. For example, drinking rainwater that collected in the footprint of a wolf, or drinking from a pond where a wolf had lapped the water, could be all it took to become a werewolf. If you ate anything a wolf drooled on, you ran the dangerous possibility of becoming a werewolf. And, eating the meat of a wolf could land you in werewolfsville.

It's even possible, according to some legends, to turn yourself into a werewolf. One way would be to perform a magic ritual, usually involving a plant called wolfsbane.

You could wear a belt made from the pelt of a wolf or the skin of an executed criminal—and this would turn you into a werewolf.

So, after you've been bitten, cursed, or magically transformed into a werewolf, what happens next? It depends on the legend. In France, the curse transforms you into a werewolf on every full moon. In some traditions you become a wolf—but you have eyes like a human. In other legends, you change into a wolf anytime you want.

No matter how you became a werewolf, the fact remains: you're now no longer human. You run through the countryside biting, attacking, and being vicious. You have become a wild animal.

How Do You Stop a Werewolf?

Obviously, the best way to avoid a werewolf is to not go into the forest on a full moon! But if you do happen to meet a werewolf, the most common weapon against it is silver. The Greek philosopher Hippocrates (460-370 B.C.) wrote about silver's healing properties. In the Middle Ages, people associated silver with the gods of the moon. So, silver became known as a weapon against werewolves. In a lot of werewolf movies, the creature is finally killed when it is shot with a silver bullet.

In the old traditions of some countries, you need to throw holy water on a werewolf to kill it. In other legends, werewolfism could be cured by love, or by stabbing the beast so that only three drops of blood come out. Sometimes a person could concoct a magical potion, often made from wolfsbane, that could stop a werewolf.

Right: Wolfsbane, a poisonous plant that can cause death. Small amounts have been used in potions designed to keep away werewolves.

Above: A snarling grey wolf.

Werewolf Sightings Throughout History

The belief that humans could share the spirit and form of animals is very, very old. On the walls of caves in what is now Turkey, there are ancient paintings of creatures that are half-leopard and half-man. These cave paintings were created by artists as far back as 6000 B.C.

Below: A man as an angry werewolf.

The earliest writing of a man becoming a wolf is in a 4,000-year-old story called the *Epic of Gilgamesh.* It is one of the earliest stories ever written. One of the characters, a shepherd, is turned by the angry gods into a wolf, "so his own shepherds now chase him and his own dogs snap at his shins."

Above: A statue of brothers Romulus and Remus. As the story goes, they were abandoned in the forest and reared by a she-wolf, then returned to build the city of Rome, Italy.

There have been many fanciful legends of children who were raised by wolves. The most famous story is about Romulus and Remus, two brothers who, according to tradition, founded the city of Rome, Italy. Romulus and Remus were raised by a wolf. This legend probably emerged as a way to make people believe that the Romans were very brave and strong.

The Greek historian Herodotus (484-425 B.C.) reported on a tribe called the Neuri, who lived in an area now within the boundaries of modern-day Poland. Herodotus retold a story he had heard that this entire tribe became wolves once a year.

The Roman poet Ovid (43 B.C. to 17 A.D.) wrote about King Lycaon of Greece, who angered the gods. To punish him, the gods turned him into a werewolf. In fact, it is from this king's name that we get the term *lycanthropy*, which is another word for werewolfism.

In the year 60 A.D., a Roman novel called *Satyricon* told the story of a man who turns into a wolf during the full moon. This seems to be the first story in which the light of a full moon changes someone into a werewolf.

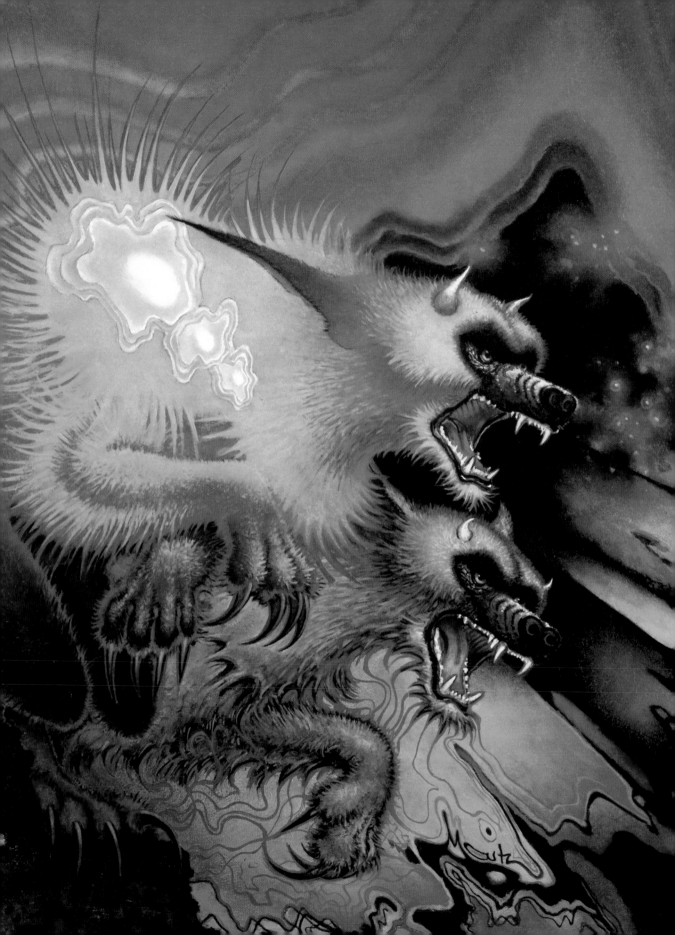

In Europe, beginning about 1100 A.D., a werewolf frenzy began. Belief in werewolves was widespread. People wrote about werewolves, talked about werewolves, and many claimed to have seen them. Trials were held for hundreds of people accused of being werewolves. Many people went to jail or were executed. Sometimes, authorities put actual wolves on trial. Frightened people imagined werewolves around every corner.

Between 1764 and 1767, the French province of Gévaudan experienced a number of animal attacks. People said the beast looked like a wolf, but that it was as big as a cow. Some people claimed it charged out of the forest and attacked children. In the course of three years, the rampaging Beast of Gévaudan killed 15 women, 6 men, and 68 children. The townspeople teamed up with professional hunters. They tried to find and kill the beast. Even the French government sent the military in an attempt to stop the rampage. Many wolves were killed, but the attacks continued. Finally, two very large wolves were killed. The attacks came to a sudden end. Historians still argue about the exact identity of the beast. Was it a wolf? Was it an escaped lion? Was it a serial killer, pretending to be a wolf? Or, perhaps, it was something else.

Some people still believed in werewolves as late as the 1800s. Sweden and Russia were at war in the 1800s, and during that time the wolf population in Sweden grew rapidly. Superstitious Swedes believed that the Russians were changing their criminals into wolves and sending them into Sweden!

Why did people believe in werewolves? What if you were superstitious, and while you were out walking in the forest, you saw someone's clothes on the ground, and then saw a wolf nearby? Would you suspect werewolfism? What if you were a hunter, and you wounded a wolf in the leg, but it got away? The next day, perhaps you saw a person walking with a limp. Would you then believe in werewolves? Many spooky tales are born from coincidences just like this.

Facing Page: Leap, by artist Don Maitz.

WEREWOLVES TODAY

According to some people, a werewolf lives today in the small town of Elkhorn, Wisconsin. For many years, Elkhorn residents have reported sightings of a large beast, the size of a man, with a wolf-like face. Some people claim it stands on its hind legs, and sometimes chases passers-by. Some people claim it might be a large coy-dog (a rare cross between a coyote and a large dog), or a wolf-dog. Or, perhaps it is something else, something more sinister—could it be a werewolf?

Medical doctors and psychiatrists today report a condition called "clinical lycanthropy." In this rare disorder, people believe they can transform into animals, often wolves. The condition is usually diagnosed as a symptom of schizophrenia. It is very rare; only about 30 cases of the disorder have ever been clinically diagnosed.

Even more rare is a disease called hypertrichosis, which is an excessive growth of hair. People with this condition have so much hair on their bodies that their skin is completely covered, making them look wolf-like.

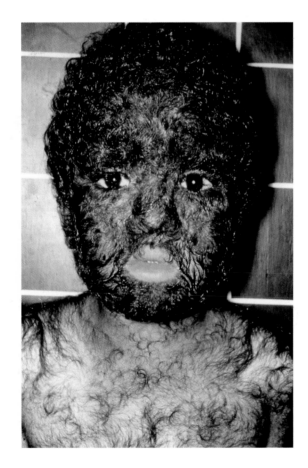

Left: A young man with hypertrichosis, a disease that causes excessive hair growth.
Facing Page: An actor walks through a city wearing a wolfman mask.

WEREWOLVES IN THE MOVIES

Werewolves have long been a popular topic for scary movies. One of the first werewolf movies was in 1913, called *The Werewolf*. Made before movies had sound, *The Werewolf* featured an actual wolf in a transformation scene.

Facing Page: Three movie posters with each movie's lead actor in werewolf makeup.
Below: Actor Jack Nicholson from the movie *Wolf*.

Probably the most famous of the early werewolf movies was *The Wolf Man*. Made in 1941, the film included many now-familiar themes: becoming a werewolf from the bite of another; transformation under a full moon; silver as the only effective weapon against a werewolf. At the end of the movie, one of the characters kills the werewolf with a silver club.

More recent movies weave the werewolf story with modern themes. *The Howling* (1981) tells the story of a TV reporter who stumbles upon a colony of werewolves. *An American Werewolf in London* (1981) is part comedy and part horror movie. It tells the story of a young tourist who is bitten by a werewolf in England. *Teen Wolf* (1985) is about a timid teenager who inherits his family's werewolf curse. It not only makes him bolder, but it makes him a better basketball player, too! *Wolf* (1994) tells the story of a man, bitten by a wolf, who slowly begins to hear better, run faster, and take charge of his life.

Underworld (2003) and *Underworld: Evolution* (2006) portray werewolves as being able to change shape at will. When they bite, they infect humans with a werewolf virus. The werewolves in these movies have a severe allergy to silver.

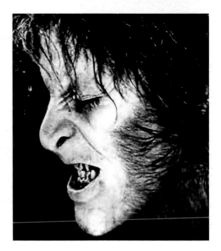

REAL-LIFE WOLVES

In real life, wolves tend to stay away from people. They usually live in packs of six or seven wolves, but sometimes have as many as 20 members. Wolves roam in their own territory, and are careful not to infringe on the land of neighboring wolf packs. Wolves hunt and eat deer, moose, elk, as well as small animals and rodents.

When wolves howl, they aren't howling at the moon, as we sometimes think. Wolves probably howl to communicate with other wolf packs. Howling is one way to make other wolf packs aware of their territory. Biologists also believe wolves howl to strengthen the bonds of the pack—kind of a group songfest.

Are wolves a danger to humans? In North America, no wolf has ever killed or seriously injured a person that we know of. However, there have been about 20 cases of wolf attacks in the last 100 years. These attacks involved a bite, a scratch, or simply running into someone and knocking them down. Usually, wolf attacks in North America are due to a person's poor judgment, such as deciding to crawl into a wolf den. When this happens, wolves feel cornered and will try to protect their pups.

Below: A wolf howls, likely communicating with other wolves.

Sometimes people feed wolves and treat them like dogs. Then wolves can lose their fear of humans. When this happens, a wolf can be very dangerous—it is a wild animal that is no longer afraid. Wolves will always be wild animals, and must be treated with respect.

In Europe and Asia, most wolf attacks have come from rabid wolves. Rabies is a disease that makes wolves much more aggressive, and much more likely to bite. People who don't have access to good medical care often die from the bite of a rabid animal. While deaths from wolf attacks in Europe and Asia are rare, there have been a few documented cases in the last 100 years.

Remember, it is only in extremely rare cases that wolves act aggressively toward humans. Normally, wolves are very frightened of humans, and will work hard to keep their distance.

Above: Two wolves from a wolf pack interact.

The Spirit of the Wolf

In ancient times, people believed that every animal had a spirit. If you were clever, you could get that spirit, and gain all the attributes of that animal. Tribal religious leaders, called shamans, believed they could get the "spirit of the wolf" by wearing the fur of a wolf. If you had the spirit of the wolf, you would become braver, stronger, and more intelligent.

In Viking times, around 900 A.D., fierce warriors called *berserkers* put on wolf pelts before battle. They believed the pelts made them stronger, faster, and more vicious. Whether or not this was true, opposing armies were often terrified at the sight of hoards of Viking berserkers charging at them dressed in wolf pelts.

Another example of the wolf spirit is seen in the Viking story *Ingiald.* According to the tale, King Aunund had a son who was timid, shy, and afraid all the time. But after eating the heart of a wolf, he became the bravest of warriors.

Sometimes simple words created confusion. In ancient Scandinavia, the word *vargr* can mean wolf, godless person, or criminal. This created confusion for some people. Was the vargr a werewolf, or just a lawbreaker? People in countries being attacked by fierce Viking warriors often called the invaders "wolves." When the battle was over, were the attackers Vikings or werewolves?

Below: The head of a snarling *Canis Lupus,* a grey wolf.

Above: A Roman standard-bearer and horn player wear wolf pelts at a historical reenactment. Soldiers from many different lands wore wolf pelts to make themselves look vicious and strong.

WHY WEREWOLVES?

What is it about werewolf legends that fascinate us? Why, after thousands of years, do we still love the story of the werewolf? Throughout history, farmers and ranchers learned to hate wolves, because wolves often attacked and ate farm animals. Wolves were seen as savage and evil, preying on sheep and other defenseless animals. Actually, the wolves were simply doing what wolves do. They weren't being evil; they were just looking for food, as all animals do (including humans). But in many places, the farmers and ranchers hunted and killed wolves in order to protect their farm animals. In some countries, like the United States, people hunted down wolves until they were almost extinct.

In Europe during the Middle Ages, murderers and other vicious criminals were called "wolves." The term represents the belief that humans are sometimes responsible for animal-like acts. The wolf represents the idea that humans can sometimes commit acts of terrible violence on each other. Sometimes, humans can do savage things. There have always been people capable of doing unspeakable violence. There have always been murderers and serial killers. Perhaps people began to believe in werewolves because we don't like to think humans can be so brutal. Maybe werewolves fascinate us because they remind us that humans can sometimes be very violent.

Whatever the reason, werewolf stories will continue to be with us… especially at night, in the forest, when there is a full moon.

Below: A United States postage stamp featuring Lon Chaney, Jr., in *The Wolf Man.*

32 USA

Lon Chaney, Jr. as
THE WOLF MAN

Above: A wolf in the snow.

GLOSSARY

GYPSY
A member of a group of wandering, nomadic people. Gypsies are commonly thought to make their living through barter, fortune telling, or common labor.

HOLY WATER
Water blessed by a priest, used for spiritual cleansing and purification.

MIDDLE AGES
The period of European history from about the year 500 to about 1500.

PELT
An undressed animal skin still having its hair or fur.

RABIES
A disease caused by a virus that affects the central nervous system (brain and spinal cord) of mammals, including humans. Rabies causes excessive saliva, abnormal behavior, and eventual paralysis and death. People can be exposed to rabies when bitten by an infected wild or domestic animal.

SCHIZOPHRENIA
A chronic, severe, and disabling brain disorder. People with schizophrenia can experience hallucinations, delusions, paranoia, and disordered thinking. These experiences can make sufferers fearful and withdrawn.

SHAMAN
A tribal person who acts as a medium between the natural and spiritual worlds. Shamans work to cure illness, foretell the future, and control events.

WITCH
A woman claiming to have supernatural powers. Witches are often considered to be old, ugly hags who use their powers in hateful ways, but this is an unfair stereotype.

WOLFSBANE
A variety of poisonous herb plants. Wolfsbane was given its name when it was used to kill wolves in attempts to rid them from an area. The plant was added to meat that was used as bait.

Above: A wolf pup born in Yellowstone National Park. Wolves, hunted to extinction in the park, were reintroduced in 1995 and 1996. They now number over 300 in the area.

INDEX

Above: A wolf near Wyoming's Yellowstone National Park.